Who Is
Cristiano Ronaldo?

Who Is
Cristiano Ronaldo?

by James Buckley Jr.

illustrated by Gregory Copeland

Penguin Workshop

To the Renegades, who keep me young
as we all try to "be like Ronaldo"—JB

PENGUIN WORKSHOP
An Imprint of Penguin Random House LLC, New York

Copyright © 2022 by Penguin Random House LLC. All rights reserved.
Published by Penguin Workshop, an imprint of Penguin Random House LLC, New York.
PENGUIN and PENGUIN WORKSHOP are trademarks of Penguin Books Ltd.
WHO HQ & Design is a registered trademark of Penguin Random House LLC.
Printed in the USA.

Visit us online at www.penguinrandomhouse.com.

Library of Congress Cataloging-in-Publication Data is available upon request.

ISBN 9780593226346 (paperback)   10 9 8 7 6 5 4 3 2 1 WOR
ISBN 9780593226353 (library binding)   10 9 8 7 6 5 4 3 2 1 WOR

Contents

Who Is Cristiano Ronaldo?

The world's greatest soccer player was crying. He was not sad. He was shedding tears of joy. At a star-studded ceremony, Cristiano Ronaldo had just won the 2013 Ballon d'Or (French for "Golden Ball"), a trophy given to the year's top player. He had won the award before, in 2008, but it had been five long years since he had taken home this important honor. This time, he did not come onto the stage alone. His three-year-old son, Cristiano Jr., had scampered up to follow his dad.

Tears flowed as Cristiano spoke in Portuguese, his native language. He thanked his mother, Dolores, and his family. He thanked his teammates and coaches. And for the first time on any stage, he tearfully thanked his son for being in his life.

For soccer fans, seeing Cristiano Ronaldo cry was not that unusual. For a decade, he had been part of some of the greatest teams and championships in world soccer, first for Sporting Lisbon in Portugal, then for Manchester United in England. Since 2009, he had been with Real (say: ray-AHL) Madrid in Spain. He had helped his teams take home trophies that brought tears of joy. He had also wept in disappointment when he could not help his national team from Portugal do the same.

Why all the tears for a game? For billions of people around the world, soccer is much more than a game. For Cristiano Ronaldo, too, it is an obsession. From almost as soon as he could walk, he had a burning desire to be the best in the game. It took a lot of hard work, a lot of talent, and a bit of luck, but now, on this stage in Switzerland, he could say that he had made it.

On the awards show stage, Cristiano stood proudly with his son by his side. They were like an island amid a sea of cheering fans. His story, however, begins on another island entirely.

CHAPTER 1
Island Kid Turns Pro

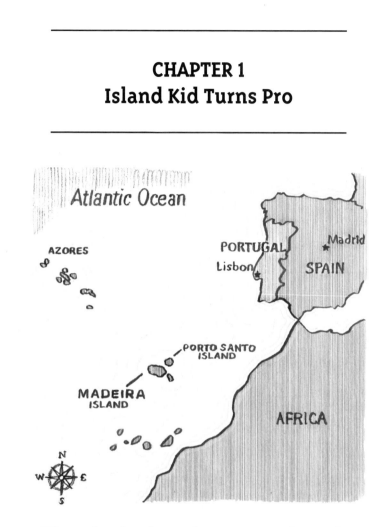

The island of Madeira is in the Atlantic Ocean, about 620 miles from the coast of Portugal. Madeira is a region of Portugal.

Cristiano Ronaldo dos Santos Aveiro was born on Madeira on February 5, 1985. His mother, Dolores dos Santos, chose the name Cristiano. His father, José Dinis, chose Ronaldo, after Ronald Reagan, the American president at the time, and a man José Dinis admired. For most of his life, Cristiano has been known just by his first two names, which is not unusual for people from Portugal.

Cristiano was the youngest of four children. The family lived in a three-room house with a tin roof in a poor part of the island's biggest city, Funchal. Soccer was a huge part of Cristiano's life from when he was very young. José Dinis worked as the equipment manager for a local soccer club called Andorinha (Portuguese for "the Swallows"). He took care of the uniforms, known as the "kit," the balls, and even the grass on the team's fields.

Once Cristiano finally got his own ball, it almost never left him. "He slept with his ball, it never left his side. It was always under his arm—wherever he went, it went with him," remembered his godfather, Fernando Sousa. Once when Cristiano brought the ball to school with him, a teacher told him he was making a mistake. She told him that the ball would never feed him; he had to put it aside and learn his lessons.

He played most often in the street, because their neighborhood had no fields. He and his friends would form goals with rocks or rags, and they had to move out of the way quickly when cars came by. From the first time he touched the ball, Cristiano was something special. He could dribble past anyone. He made moves that only older players would try. Cristiano followed his father to work sometimes and tried to play with the older kids on the junior team. By the time the young player was nine years old, he had joined Andorinha.

As great as he was at soccer, Cristiano was still very young. He cried often—when he missed a goal, when his team lost, when the ball wasn't

passed to him. In fact, one of his nicknames on the team was "Crybaby."

His teammates gave him another nickname: Abelhinha, which means "little bee" in Portuguese. They saw him zipping around like a buzzing insect as he played.

José Dinis often came to watch Cristiano's games. Dolores watched, too, but she later said she was too nervous. She did not want to see her son get hurt!

Cristiano's skills were now being noticed by other teams. A larger youth club called Nacional wanted him to join. In 1995, Andorinha was given twenty soccer balls and two sets of team uniforms to release Cristiano so he could join the other team.

He was not with Nacional very long. When he was twelve, a pro soccer club called Sporting Lisbon, in the capital of Portugal, asked him to try out. They had heard stories of this amazing island player who was tall and skinny, fast and dedicated. Top pro teams in Europe often have youth academies. They pay for young players to live and train together. The hope is that many will grow up to play for the club's top teams.

At only twelve years old, Cristiano would have to leave his island home for the first time and live across the water in the city of Lisbon, far from his family.

Cristiano didn't think twice. It was a chance to keep playing the game he loved. In August 1997, he flew to Lisbon to begin his pro career.

CHAPTER 2
Moving Up

With Sporting, Cristiano soon showed he was one of the best players. The same soccer skills he had learned in Funchal's streets quickly made him a star on the Lisbon "pitch," as soccer fields are often called. Life off the field was harder, however. Cristiano was very homesick and cried almost every night. He had to take care of himself, living in a dorm with other young players. On one of many tearful phone calls back home, he complained to his mother that he had to do his own ironing! Once he spent all his lunch money on chocolate and had to write home for more.

Because he had not put any effort into

his school on Madeira, the classes he and the other players took were very difficult for him. He also spoke Portuguese with a Madeiran accent; some kids made fun of how he sounded. "It was very hard," he remembered later. "It was the most difficult time in my sporting career."

Still, he stuck with it and kept training. Staying busy helped with his homesickness. As long as he kept busy in the gym or on the practice field, he was not lonely. He would sometimes sneak out of his dorm after the lights were out to go lift weights. He was still thinner than most players and knew he had to get stronger to compete well. Keeping his body in top shape became another lifelong obsession.

"I knew I had a lot of talent, but I decided that I was going to work harder than everybody," he said. "I was going to stop playing like a kid.

I was going to train like I could be the best
in the world."

His desire to win was strong, too. He still
cried when his team lost or when things did
not go his way. "He wanted to be the best at

everything—table tennis, pool, darts, foosball, athletics—he wanted to beat every opponent. He had to win no matter what sport he was playing," said Leonel Pontes, one of the teachers at the Sporting school.

Sporting, like most clubs, has several age-level teams, such as the under-seventeens and the under-twenties. Cristiano quickly moved up the ranks. When he was just seventeen, he made it to the Sporting Lisbon team that played in the Portuguese pro league, called Primeira Liga (say: pre-MAYR-ah LEE-gah).

Cristiano played for his team in Lisbon, but also played for his country's team. He had been a member of national youth teams starting at fourteen. In 2003, he helped Portugal win a big under-twenty tournament in France. At that event, scouts from big pro clubs around the world were watching. Teams from Italy, England, and Spain had their eye on Cristiano.

CHAPTER 3
The Man at Man U

Portugal's professional league includes some fine teams and top players. But it is very small and earns much less money than leagues in bigger countries such as England or Spain. So while Cristiano was proud to play for Sporting, he knew that other teams in other leagues were his future, even if that meant playing in other countries.

In 2003, after receiving several offers, Cristiano chose to join Manchester United, in the English Premier League. "Man U," as the team is known, is one of the most famous and successful pro clubs in the world. Man U has featured some of the world's best soccer stars wearing its familiar red jerseys as the team has won dozens of major trophies.

Two Types of Teams

The best soccer players in the world play for two teams: club and national. Professional clubs play in leagues organized in just about every country in the world. Pro club players can be from any country. They sign contracts that allow them to change teams when their contracts are up. Professional players can also be "transferred" from team to team if the clubs choose. Players play hard for their team, and they can earn large salaries if they are successful.

The other type of soccer team is the national team. Each nation has teams of players at different age levels. All the players must be a citizen of that country. For example, Cristiano can only play on a national team for Portugal. He can play for a pro club anywhere in the world.

Players wear their national kit—or uniform—with pride, playing for the honor of their country at events such as championships for each continent or at the World Cup, which is held every four years.

Insignia of the Portugal national football team

To sign Cristiano, the English team paid Sporting Lisbon about $19 million, a record for a teen player. Cristiano himself would be paid two million euros (about $2.26 million today) per season by Man U. Cristiano knew that his offer from Man U was a huge opportunity for him. "I'm going to be the best in the world," he told the coaches. "And you're going to help me."

"He was like a sponge," said Man U assistant coach Mike Phelan. "He wanted more."

Trainer Mike Clegg taught Cristiano better ways of working out. The Premier League was tougher than the league in Portugal. Players were bigger. Cristiano needed more strength to play with these older and heavier players. He spent hours in the gym, lifting weights and becoming even more fit.

Man U manager Sir Alex Ferguson put pressure on Cristiano by giving him the number seven jersey. Some of Man U's most famous and successful players, including David Beckham, Eric Cantona, and George Best, had worn that number. Ferguson was showing that he expected a lot from Cristiano. (The number eventually became part of Cristiano's well-known "CR7" nickname.)

Even with Ferguson's support, Cristiano, as the second-youngest player, had to put up with some teasing from older players. They pointed out how much money he was earning and the fancy clothes he wore. And when he tried some complicated move and it didn't work, he'd hear it from the veteran players. But they did recognize his talent and welcomed him as part of the team.

While he was settling in to life in England, Cristiano still had the chance to wear the maroon jersey of his country's national team. In 2004, Portugal took part in the European Championship.

This tournament included most of the teams on the continent. That year, the final matches were played in Portugal itself. Cristiano helped Portugal win game after game. For the first time ever, Portugal reached the championship match. However, against a strong team from Greece, Portugal lost 1–0. Cristiano was very disappointed. He wanted to win in front of friends and family.

The final game in Lisbon was one of the last times his father saw him play. José Dinis was not well. Cristiano paid for his father to fly to a special clinic in London, but it was too late. José Dinis died in September 2005.

Cristiano was sad, but after the funeral on Madeira, he threw himself into his play.

For the next three seasons, 2006 through 2008, Man U was one of the best teams in the world. They won the Premier League in three straight seasons. Cristiano thrilled fans with his amazing play. He scored 66 goals in 101 games. In 2007 and 2008 he was named the Player of the Season in the Premier League.

By 2008, Cristiano and Man U had one more goal to achieve. Each year, the Union of European Football Associations (UEFA) Champions League brings together thirty-two of the top-ranked pro clubs from the continent for a final tournament. The team that wins the Champions League is considered by soccer experts to be the top club in the world. Man U had not won this event since 1999.

After beating each team in the Champions League playoffs, Man U and Cristiano reached the 2008 Champions League final against Chelsea, another team from England.

In the twenty-sixth minute of the game,

Cristiano banged in a head ball for the game's first goal. Late in the first half, Chelsea's Frank Lampard scored to tie the game. The teams played to a tie, and then no one scored in thirty minutes of extra time. The tie was broken by

a penalty-kick shootout. Incredibly, Cristiano had his shot blocked by the Chelsea goalie! However, other Man U players made their kicks and, in the end, Cristiano and his teammates hoisted the Champions League trophy!

In early 2009, the voting results for the Ballon d'Or for 2008 were announced. For the first time, Cristiano Ronaldo was the winner. That May, he and Man U lost in the Champions League final to FC Barcelona. That Spanish team was led by Lionel Messi, a player who would become Cristiano's greatest rival.

CHAPTER 4
The Big Move to Spain

In 2009, the Ronaldo-Messi rivalry got more intense. After six seasons at Man U, Cristiano felt it was time to move on. He wanted a new challenge. He found it in Spain. Real Madrid paid Man U more than $131 million to end his contract with the English team and bring him to Spain. His new Spanish team agreed to pay him more than $18 million per season, more than any other soccer player in the world. Now, Cristiano would face Messi several times a year, because Barcelona was Real Madrid's fiercest rival.

Real Madrid fans were overjoyed. On July 6, 2009, more than eighty thousand people packed the famous Santiago Bernabéu Stadium in the city of Madrid to welcome him.

Lionel Messi (1987–)

Lionel Messi has become one of the greatest soccer players of all time.

At thirteen, Messi traveled far away from his home in Rosario, Argentina, to join the legendary youth academy at FC Barcelona in Spain. By the time he was sixteen, he was playing for Barcelona's adult team in La Liga (say: LAH LEE-gah), the professional league in Spain. He helped them win ten league championships and four Champions League titles. In 2021, he helped Argentina win the Copa América, the championship of South America.

In 2012, he became Barcelona's all-time leading scorer when he knocked in his 233rd career goal. By early 2022, he had scored more than 750 goals for club and country. In 2021, he joined Paris Saint-Germain, a team in France.

"My dream of playing for Real Madrid has come true," he told them from the field. "I didn't expect this. It's amazing!" Then he led

the fans in the traditional team cheer, "One, two, three—*Hala, Madrid! Hala, Madrid!*" which means "Forward, Madrid!"

In the summer of 2010, Cristiano made a surprise announcement that had nothing to do with sports. He had become a father. Cristiano Jr. was born on June 17 in the United States. Cristiano did not tell anyone who the mother of his son was.

"I think I should keep that to myself," he said. He has also said that when Cristiano Jr. is older, he will tell his son the whole story. Partly because he did not know his father as well as he wanted, Cristiano really wanted a son of his own. "It was a dream of mine to be a father, a young father," he said, and his dream came true when he was twenty-five.

He spread the news of his son in a new way. Not long before Cristiano Jr. was born, Cristiano started his Twitter account. Fans and reporters were quick to follow him. He shared news of his life and his son with his fans in tweets.

In 2013, Cristiano had one of his best seasons. He scored sixty-nine goals for Real Madrid and Portugal. He became the first Real Madrid player ever to score thirty goals in three straight seasons. And he tied for most career goals scored for Portugal, with forty-seven. Messi had also had a great year. It would be up to the voters to see who would be named the world's best player.

The soccer world gathered in Zurich, Switzerland, for the annual awards event. When the envelope was opened for the Ballon d'Or, Cristiano's name was inside. He had won his second Golden Ball! His son joined him on the stage as Cristiano proudly thanked his family and teammates.

CHAPTER 5
The Magician in Madrid

In May 2014, Cristiano led Real Madrid to the final of the Champions League. The Spanish club had won this important tournament nine times.

It was seeking its tenth, which it called La Décima ("the tenth" in English). Real Madrid faced its cross-city rival, Atlético Madrid. Real tied the game very late at 1–1. In extra time, Cristiano and his team scored three goals. Cristiano's penalty-kick goal made the final score 4–1 and set off a huge celebration. The win was extra special because the game was played in Lisbon, Portugal, where his

family and friends were all able to watch.

Later that summer, things did not go as well in the World Cup. Cristiano had a knee injury, but he kept playing. Portugal lost to Germany and could only manage a tie with the United States. It was not enough to advance, and Portugal went home early.

Cristiano did not win a World Cup, but he did win another important award. In 2015, he was named the world's most charitable athlete by the website DoSomething.org. That year, he had sent almost $8 million to help victims of an earthquake in Nepal, a country in the Himalayan mountains of Central Asia. This was nothing new for Cristiano. As soon as he began earning a large salary playing professional soccer, Cristiano had started giving much of it away. He bought houses for his mother and his family, along with a new Porsche for Dolores. In 2020, he and his teammates also donated millions of dollars to help with COVID-19 relief. Over his career, he has even paid medical bills for some of his fans.

Cristiano has purposely never gotten a tattoo so that he can continue to donate blood regularly. In many countries, having a tattoo can mean you are not allowed to donate.

"My father always taught me that when you help other people, then God will give you double," said Cristiano. "And that's what really happened to me. When I have helped people who are in need, God has helped me more."

In the summer of 2016, Cristiano led Portugal in another European Championship tournament. As it had in 2004, the team reached the championship game. However, about eight minutes into the championship game against France, a French player ran into Cristiano. The Portuguese star fell to the ground, holding his knee. He got up in a few minutes, but could not continue to play. He was carried to the locker room.

Cristiano was off the field, but not out of the game. After regulation time, the score tied, Cristiano returned, with his knee wrapped with ice, to the sidelines to cheer on his team. He helped coaches with strategy and encouraged teammates. Late in extra time with the score still tied, Portugal sent in Cristiano's teammate Eder to play forward. "Cristiano told me that I would score when I came on," Eder said. Cristiano's prediction came true. Eder scored, and Portugal won the European Championship for the first time! As team captain, Cristiano raised the trophy high as his teammates jumped for joy. And yes, he was crying.

"This is the greatest moment of my career," he said. "Tears of anger at the injury, and then [tears of] joy at the triumph. This trophy goes out to all the Portuguese people!"

CHAPTER 6
World's Best

Cristiano shed more tears of joy in 2017, when he became the father of twins, Mateo and Eva Maria. Again, the identity of their mother was not revealed. Later that same year, Cristiano's girlfriend, Georgiana Rodriguez, gave birth to their daughter, Alana. He was now the proud father of four kids.

In 2018, after winning a fifth Ballon d'Or, Cristiano said, "I'm the best player in history. I've never seen anyone better than me. I have always thought that."

Later that summer, Cristiano led Real Madrid to its third straight Champions League title. At that point, he decided it was time for another change. He looked for another world to conquer, and he found it in Italy. Cristiano led his new team, Juventus, to the 2019 Italian Serie A league title. He became the first player with league championships in England, Spain, and Italy.

In Italy, Cristiano kept right on with his plan to help others. He put his 2013 Ballon d'Or trophy up for auction. The sale raised more than $750,000, which he donated to the Make-a-Wish Foundation.

In 2018, a woman accused him of assault in 2009 in Las Vegas. "I firmly deny the accusations against me," he said. Police did not find enough evidence. He was not charged with any crime. Then, in early 2019, he did admit to a crime. He had not paid enough taxes in Spain. He paid a fine of more than $20 million.

In March 2020, the world soccer season had to pause for the coronavirus pandemic. After teams started playing again, Cristiano led Juventus to another Serie A championship.

He also continued to play for Portugal.

In September 2021, Cristiano scored his 110th goal for his country. That gave him the all-time record among male players, topping the mark of Ali Daei of Iran, who had 109. In January 2022, Cristiano was given a FIFA Special Award in honor of this record-breaking achievement. (Seventeen women have reached 100, with Canada's Christine Sinclair on top with 188.)

In the summer of 2021, Cristiano made a move again, but this time back to a familiar place. He signed a contract to return to Manchester United, where he had first become a superstar. The team gave him his number seven jersey, and fans were thrilled to have him back.

Meanwhile, Cristiano Jr. was playing for one of the youth teams of Manchester United. Like his father, he has dreams of soccer greatness. And he knows that only hard work and dedication to be the "best in the world" will do.

On the soccer field and off, Cristiano is one of the most famous people in the world. As of early 2022, he had more than 96 million Twitter followers. He also has more followers on Instagram than any other person! Even with all the awards and championships he has won, Cristiano is determined to keep playing hard and winning even more. The more he wins, the more people he can help. What else would a hero do?

Timeline of Cristiano Ronaldo's Life

1985 — Born February 5, in Funchal, Madeira, Portugal

1997 — Leaves home to join Sporting Lisbon

2003 — Signed contract with Manchester United in English Premier League

2007 — Named top player in Premier League

2008 — Wins UEFA Champions League with Manchester United

— Wins first Ballon d'Or as world's top player

2009 — Joins Real Madrid in Spain's La Liga

2010 — Son Cristiano Jr. is born

2013 — Wins second Ballon d'Or as world's top player

2014 — Leads Real Madrid to first of three straight Champions League titles

2016 — With Portugal, wins European Championship

2017 — Children Mateo, Eva Maria, and Alana born

— Wins fifth Ballon d'Or

2018 — Joins Juventus in Italy's Serie A

2021 — Returns to play for Manchester United

— Becomes all-time leading male international scorer with 110 goals

Timeline of the World

1985 — Explorer Robert Ballard finds the wreckage of the RMS *Titanic* deep under the Atlantic Ocean

1991 — The World Wide Web is first used by the public

1994 — Former longtime political prisoner Nelson Mandela is elected as the first Black president of South Africa

1997 — The first Harry Potter book is published in England

— Pathfinder becomes the first rover successfully landed on Mars

2000 — Tiger Woods wins the British Open with a record score and becomes youngest player to win all four of golf's Grand Slam events

2003 — The Iraq War begins

2005 — Hurricane Katrina causes great damage and loss of life in the southern United States

2008 — Barack Obama is elected as the first African American US president

2016 — Great Britain votes to leave the European Union, a process called "Brexit"

2020 — The virus that causes COVID-19 spreads around the world, disrupting everyday life and eventually killing more than five million people

Bibliography

*Books for young readers

*Apps, Roy. *Cristiano Ronaldo. Sporting Heroes.* New York:
Franklin Watts, 2017.

Balague, Guillem. *Cristiano Ronaldo: The Biography.* London:
Orion, 2015.

Caioli, Luca. *Ronaldo.* Rev. ed. London: Icon Books, 2018.

*Nicks, Erin. *Cristiano Ronaldo. World's Greatest Soccer Players.*
Minneapolis: SportsZone, 2020.

*Spragg, Iain. *Cristiano Ronaldo: The Ultimate Fan Book.*
London: Welbeck/Carlton, 2017.